simple Solutions

Bedrooms

simpleSolutions

Bedrooms

COLEEN CAHILL

Foreword by Timothy Drew,
Managing Editor, *Home Magazine*

FRIEDMAN/FAIRFAX

Library of Congress Cataloging-in-Publication Data:

Cahill, Coleen.

  Bedrooms / Coleen Cahill.
     p. cm. – (Simple solutions)
  Includes bibliographical references and index.
  ISBN 1-58663-165-9 (alk. paper)
     1. Bedrooms. 2. Interior decoration. I. Title. II. Simple solutions

  NK2117.B4 C29 2001
  747.7'7—dc21

2001033620

EDITOR: Sharyn Rosart
ART DIRECTOR: Jeff Batzli
DESIGNER: Midori Nakamura
PHOTO EDITOR: Paquita Bass
PRODUCTION MANAGER: Richela Fabian Morgan

Color separations by Fine Arts Repro House Co., Ltd.
Printed in China by C & C Offset Printing Co., Ltd

1 3 5 7 9 10 8 6 4 2

Distributed by Sterling Publishing Company, Inc.
387 Park Avenue South
New York, NY 10016
Distributed in Canada by Sterling Publishing
Canadian Manda Group
One Atlantic Avenue, Suite 105
Toronto, Ontario, Canada M6K 3E7
Distributed in Australia by
Capricorn Link (Australia) Pty Ltd.
P.O. Box 704
Windsor, NSW 2756, Australia

Acknowledgments

Thank you to Tim Drew from *Home Magazine* for contributing the foreword, and to Paquita Bass, Lori Epstein, and Kate Perry for their help with the photography for this book. Special thanks to my editor, Sharyn Rosart.

Contents

Foreword

"It is a delicious moment, certainly, that of being well nestled in bed and feeling that you shall drop gently to sleep." Leigh Hunt's observation neatly describes the whole purpose of the bedroom—to provide an environment of comfort and repose where we can put away the cares of the day and slip easily into sweet slumber. This would seem a fairly straightforward prescription of what a bedroom needs to be, but through the decades we've made substantial additions to our expectations.

In our Walter Mitty–like daydreams, many of us have at one time or another wished to be a knight of the Round Table, Louis XIV, or some other historical figure. But we can be grateful that no fairy godmother granted us that misguided wish, as many of the creature comforts to which we've become accustomed would be lost. The everyday knight could look forward to a fitful night's sleep on a crude straw pallet. And while Versailles may have been the last word in seventeenth-century opulence, every morning, a motley crew of favored courtiers barged in to get Louis out of bed and dressed. What's more, there was not the slightest prospect of air-conditioning or central heating, much less a hot shower. Even the highest members of society did not experience comfort and privacy at the levels that we do today.

In fact, not so very long ago, in the mid-twentieth century, the bedroom was a fairly uncomplicated affair. It needed to accommodate an appropriate bed—a double bed for Mom and Dad, twin beds for the kids—and a dresser or two. Closet space favored the less is more concept, and the bathroom was located down the hall. Though the decor may have varied according to taste, the basic elements remained the same.

But technology has enormously expanded our ability to create living spaces exactly attuned to our personal requirements and tastes. We can now take it for granted that certain amenities will be available. And in the last decade or so, we've seen the phenomenon of what is called "cocooning," an underlying desire to make our homes a haven from the pressures and stress of the outside world. Within that family haven, we've incorporated not only open, or public, spaces where we share time with family members and entertain guests, but also more private spaces where we can spend quiet, reflective time. And, as the ultimate private space, the bedroom has evolved into a personal sanctum sanctorum. It has become a retreat where we can truly unwind, relax, and recharge our batteries. After all, it is where we go to recover from each day's activities as well as where we get ready for each new day.

Faced with such high expectations, you might feel that designing a bedroom is a daunting task, but with Coleen Cahill's *Simple Solutions: Bedrooms* in hand, you will have an easy-to-use road map to lead you through the process. On every page, practical tips and useful ideas will help keep you on track with your decision-making. And the sheer number and variety of photographs that illustrate the concepts discussed offer endless visual inspiration. With so much helpful guidance in planning your own perfect bedroom, it's safe to say that you'll never again have to get up on the wrong side of the bed.

Timothy Drew
Managing Editor, *Home Magazine*

Introduction

The bedroom occupies a unique role in our daily lives. It is the place where we greet each morning and where we find refuge at the end of each day. If the kitchen is the hub of the modern home, then the bedroom is a personal haven, a place for each member of the family to recharge before emerging again to participate in the lively exchange that marks daily life.

Our bedrooms offer a peek into our private worlds—they reflect how we want to live when no one else is around. Nevertheless, when we invite others in, our bedrooms become public expressions of our private selves, and they chronicle the cycles of our lives.

Many of our most vivid childhood memories reside in bedrooms past, from the universally beloved ritual of the bedtime story to nights spent whispering to a sibling in the next bed long after lights out. Pillow fights, sleepovers, homework, dreams, and even nightmares—all these may have formed part of the bedroom's emotional and psychological landscape. Indeed, the bedroom, especially for a child, is much more than just a place to sleep: it is at once playground, classroom, and launching pad for dreams—of both the daytime and nighttime variety.

As children move into adolescence, bedrooms take on a unique importance. As they go through the not-always-easy process of growing up and becoming independent, teenagers may begin to crave privacy. Teenagers also typically view their rooms as one of the rare places where they can truly express themselves. In fact, many people's first real efforts at decorating took place in their teenage bedrooms—though it may have been as simple as pinning up posters of a favorite band or sports team. And for most teenagers, the bedroom offers a personal refuge from an increasingly complex world.

It's not just teenagers who need a place to retreat. Many of us view our bedrooms as private refuges. In the bedroom, where we are surrounded by our most intimate possessions, the demands of the day fade away at last. That feeling of finding a haven is so comforting that many bedrooms today are being designed to be far more than mere places to sleep. Just like our younger counterparts, we yearn to spend more time in our bedrooms—builders and designers are obliging us with master suites that may include spa-like bathrooms, adjoining sitting rooms, and distinct dressing areas. Yet even without a lot of space or a big budget, creating a bedroom that satisfies both body and soul is within everyone's reach.

A truly personal space, the bedroom is the perfect place to explore your own style. The bedroom is a contained space that is usually removed from the public areas of the home, so you don't have to worry about extending the decorating theme into nearby rooms. Your vision and creativity are the only limitations.

As with any room, the first step is to think about your particular needs. Although not as functionally demanding as the kitchen or bathroom, your bedroom probably still has to do at least several jobs well, including providing a place for restful sleep and storing whatever items you want to keep close at hand. In addition, it may serve as a home office or entertainment center. You may want to start by asking yourself some questions. How do you relax? What are your bedtime rituals? Will you spend time in the bedroom during the day or evening? Is the entire family welcome, or is it invitation only? Will you want to include entertainment options such as a television or computer—or do you view the bedroom as a place of peace and quiet?

Once you have considered these questions, you are ready for the details. The bedroom's primary task is to provide a comfortable place for sleeping. Selecting a bed is one of the most critical decisions you'll make when planning a new bedroom or refreshing an existing one. The bed is the centerpiece of the bedroom, and will anchor the rest of the furnishings in the room. Fortunately, there is an endless variety of beds that combine comfort with style: spend some time exploring all the options until you find a bed that truly suits you. Then you'll be ready to think about color, fabric, and furnishings.

Adequate storage is another critical component in a well-designed bedroom. Careful planning is the key to ending up with storage solutions that meet your needs. Keep in mind that it's not just clothes and shoes that need to be stowed. Extra linens, books, and CDs are just a few of the items that often end up in the bedroom. Think about combining built-in storage with freestanding pieces, like a wardrobe, that will provide added flexibility. A good way to get started on your storage plans is with a list of everything that needs to be stored. Then think about who needs access to these items and how often.

The demands placed on bedrooms that do double duty as dens or home offices are even greater. This is often the case with guest rooms. As a room that serves more than one person, and often has a "day job," the guest room has to be ready to welcome visitors of all ages, offering them a comfortable place to rest for a night or two. Again, the bed will set the tone. Consider whether you need a double bed to accommodate couples, or whether two twin beds will suffice, providing even greater flexibility. If the guest room also serves as an office or hobby area, a daybed or Murphy bed may be the best choice. Keep in mind that a guest room should be easy to settle into, not to mention easy to clean up.

Whether you're building a new home or updating an existing bedroom, you'll face many decorative and functional decisions. *Simple Solutions: Bedrooms* will help guide you through the process. You'll find solutions to practical problems plus ideas that will inspire you to take a fresh look at how to make the bedroom a truly personal and restorative space. Use this book to create the bedroom of your dreams.

Coleen Cahill

The Master Retreat

he concept of transforming the master bedroom into a private retreat is a welcome trend for those seeking the ultimate in **relaxation**. The key is to make the space a pleasant room in which to spend time. Major amenities such as an adjoining spa bathroom or sitting room require planning up front, but almost any room can accommodate an area that is perfect for reclining, reading, or **daydreaming**. Evaluate the space, select a spot to place some comfortable furnishings, and voilà—your retreat awaits.

bright ideas

- Private terrace or deck
- His-and-hers walk-in closets
- Built-ins to stow stereo and TV
- Dimmer switches to control lighting

Built-in bookshelves flanking a fireplace give this master bedroom the air of a cozy den. Two over-stuffed, slipcovered chairs and a matching sofa positioned around the generously sized coffee table encourage relaxation. ➲

An airy bedroom with a tranquil neutral palette becomes a haven with two distinct areas for relaxing: a chaise takes advantage of the natural light and windows at one end of the room, while a cozy conversation area has been set up with two chairs and a small table in between.

Sheer panels soften the natural light, creating a soothing ambience, while at night, the shades can be lowered for more privacy.

An appreciation for the masters of mid-century modern design can coexist beautifully with a desire for relaxation, as this minimal master bedroom proves. Positioned to take advantage of both the expanse of windows and the simple fireplace, the Le Corbusier chaise and Eileen Gray table make both a style statement and a comfortable resting site. ↻

The best modern pieces combine form with function: the chaise and table are both adjustable for comfort.

Architectural interest and natural beauty vie for attention in this master retreat, in which the bed is the central locale from which to relax and enjoy the view. Floor-to-ceiling windows afford a panoramic view of the outdoors. A fireplace with a raised hearth allows the flames to be appreciated while the viewer is lounging in bed. ➲

A slender counter with three drawers beneath spans the window around the corner, creating a floating vanity that does not obstruct the view.

A spacious, light-filled master suite mixes upholstered and wood furnishings together to create a cottage-comfortable environment for sleep and leisure—an abundance of seating makes the room perfect for relaxed entertaining, too. A sizable patterned rug draws the conversation area together, helping to make it distinct from the sleeping area. ↻

The cheerful print of the bed linens is reprised on several of the upholstered pieces, providing a sense of continuity. Red pillows and a wing chair add a splash of color. The large table keeps books and snacks within easy reach. ♋

Appropriate lighting adds to the relaxed ambience in any space: here, spots can be positioned to illuminate the reading and writing areas.

A passion for books is evident in this library-like master suite. The proportions of the elongated room help create a separate space for the reading area, where an overstuffed chair and ottoman make for a cozy spot to relax with a book, and a writing desk offers a convenient surface if one is moved to pick up a pen. ➲

Sitting Room

ne of the simplest yet most effective ways to increase the amoun of relaxation in your life is to create a pleasant **spot to sit**, and then use it. A window seat designed to take advantage of the view is one such perfect place. When built-ins are not an option, a window may still serve as the perfect backdrop for a relaxed seating area, and freestanding upholstered pieces offer comfort and **flexibility**. Since a bedroom often has to accommodate several large items of furniture, it's a good idea to experiment with layouts on paper before investing in seating.

bright ideas

▶ Window seat storage

▶ Seasonal slipcovers that coordinate with bed linens

▶ Wheels and casters for mobility

An arched window turns this window seat into a focal point of the room. A pair of pillows make it a comfortable place to enjoy a cup of coffee and a glimpse of the outdoors. ➲

Adequat lighting can b a challenge i a small spac this brass floc lamp with a adjustable arr is a handsom solutior

An alcove with windows on three sides is large enough for a comfortable chair and ottoman, creating an inviting nook in which to pass a peaceful moment. Simple blue-bordered window shades control light and privacy. ↺

A breezy bay was added to this bedroom specifically to create a place for a relaxed seating area. The unadorned windows and high ceiling make the space feel open and airy. The chairs are just right for an intimate chat or a quiet moment of savoring the view. The space is large enough to be versatile: a sofa or chaise could fit in comfortably. ⊂

Fabric shades are both functional and decorative, and can easily be adjusted depending on the time of day.

A sunny corner is transformed into a generous seating area with upholstered foam cushions and plenty of pillows to provide support. Built-in window seats are an excellent solution when space is limited or when furniture would be too intrusive. ⋒

Even a small nook can offer sufficient space for a comfortable bedroom perch. Here, a recessed window is transformed into an inviting niche with a comfy seat cushion, small pillows, and a fabric skirt that creates a tailored look. ◖

Rather than clutter the simple space with storage or entertainment pieces, this bedroom's inhabitants selected an overstuffed chair and ottoman suitable for peaceful reclining. The small wooden table to the left of the chair provides an ideal resting place for a book or a cup of tea. ◗

*Breathtaking views
and the absence of
privacy issues allow for
uncovered windows—
these elegant draperies
are for effect only.*

A stunning water view called for the corner of this bedroom to be turned into a seating area. Free-standing furniture can be moved around to take advantage of the view. The telescope allows for close inspection of the night sky. ☋

Alcoves & Adjoining Rooms

n adjoining bathroom, sitting room, or dressing area allows the bedroom's ambience to be extended beyond the actual sleeping area. Such a setup offers a decorating **opportunity**, allowing you to create a relationship between two connected spaces. Simple floor and wall treatments can intensify the distinctiveness of or help to unify the areas. Consider whether you want complete privacy or merely a **quiet niche** before exploring options for closing off adjoining rooms.

bright ideas

▶ Sandblasted glass offers privacy without blocking light

▶ Pocket doors maximize floor and wall space

▶ Antique doors and door frames add character

To complement the Asian-inspired decor of this bedroom, sliding shoji panels with a semitranslucent pattern were chosen in place of a traditional bathroom door. The mix of materials and textures—paper, stone, wood, fabric— brings the two rooms into a tactile, sensuous whole. ☊

Shoji-style sliding screens provide a simple way to separate the master bedroom from an adjoining sitting room. Closing the doors creates privacy and makes the sleeping area cozier, but light can continue to pass between the two spaces so the airy feeling of the room is not compromised. ↻

Even a small, architecturally unremarkable space can be transformed into a calm bedroom retreat. This room's alcove opening provides a simple transition into the dressing room. The clean right angles of the doorway reflect the simple lines found on the headboard, the cube-like wall sconces, and the sizable wardrobe. ☉

Complementary shades of taupe, ivory, and brown in the bed linens, draperies, and furniture warm up the room while preserving its tranquil feeling.

Extra-wide molding is a simple solution for adding character and charm to new construction.

A traditionally styled bedroom achieves a relaxed luminosity via a sunny alcove framed with crisp white molding. Wicker rockers with patterned cushions bring a touch of the garden indoors. ♋

A Space Apart

Wide-open areas present tremendous design possibilities. With plenty of space to accommodate various **activities** from sleeping to bathing, you can create a room that truly suits your way of living. Introducing boundaries is a simple way to define and improve the **functionality** of a large space. Divisions create an opportunity to incorporate interesting architectural or decorative elements, too.

bright ideas

▶ Call upon architectural details to demarcate space

▶ Use color and flooring to define zones

▶ Employ movable screens for flexibility

A permanent divider preserves the expansive feeling of this woodsy suite while delineating a distinct area for the spa. To achieve a sense of unity, the three-quarter wall was executed in the same pine as the rest of the room's exposed woodwork. ➲

Stopping the divider a few feet shy of the center beam allows light and air to circulate.

Note that a divider can offer an additional surface for displaying art and other treasures.

Texture is the key element in this Japanese-inspired bedroom. A sleek wooden wall divides the sleeping area from the dressing space. Light and dark woods contrast to stunning effect, while the blond divider blends seamlessly with the woven ceiling. ☯

keep in mind

- ☐ Bathing areas require more than plumbing: ventilation, adequate lighting, and appropriate flooring must all be taken into account

- ☐ Sound in a large open space will travel— explore soundproofing ideas, including carpeting

- ☐ Heat rises; a ceiling fan is a simple way to keep air circulating

Modern and traditional tastes meet in this loft-style room, in which a simple wall hugs a snug sleeping area. The divider was designed to accommodate a double bed and two sizable dressers that serve as night tables. Matching reading lamps are mounted directly on the divider. ☁

Minimalism is the key to serenity in this room; all extraneous elements have been removed. A simple white wall that seems to float in space serves as a headboard for the double bed. Small glass shelves set into either side of the bed provide a resting spot for a clock or glass of water. Recessed bulbs in the ceiling take the place of bedside lamps. ↻

Controls for the lights have been built into the headboard.

High ceilings permitted this room to be divided vertically. A loft space above the sleeping area allows for additional storage and a dressing area. Access is provided by a staircase that is as spare as it is functional. ☺

Cozying Up

A snug space can be a cozy **refuge**, so don't ignore the potential of attics, dens, or other small rooms. What these rooms are lacking in size they make up for with **personality** and charm. Converting unused spaces into bedrooms makes a lot of sense for growing families; it is also a way of accommodating overnight guests. The dimensions of a quirky space can present some challenges, but there are plenty of clever ways to **get the most** out of a tight corner.

The top floor of this old home has been converted into a hospitable guest bedroom. Simple furnishings with clean lines fill but do not crowd the space. A built-in cupboard that fits under the angled wall and a wooden trunk placed at the end of the bed are attractive, space-saving storage solutions. ➲

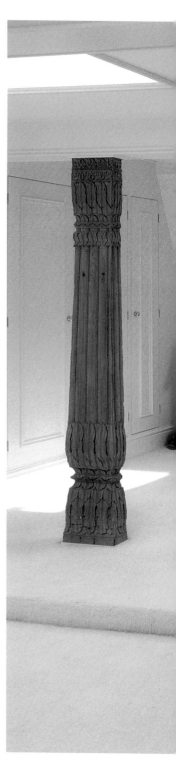

Note the built-in shelf that wraps around the room, providing a display surface.

An all-white scheme makes even a low-ceilinged attic room seem expansive. Interesting structural details are highlighted, particularly the beautifully carved wooden pillars, which define space, and the window niche, which serves as an architectural headboard for the bed. ☉

The narrow dimensions of this guest bedroom present a layout challenge. A double bed just fits, while two small shelves on either side serve as night tables. The trunk at the end of the bed provides storage as well as a surface on which guests can rest a suitcase. ☊

Wall-mounted light fixtures are a must in a tight space such as this.

This dormer bedroom packs a lot into a small space: the window behind the bed was added to bring more light into the room, and built-in shelves create much-needed storage out of otherwise unused space. ◖

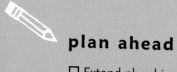
A bolder sensibility rejects the all-white solution to a small space, opting instead to draw attention to color and pattern. Two twin beds are nestled against a low wall and framed by an exposed beam painted bright green. Color-coordinated linens along with a rustic table and lamp create an overall effect that is fun and cheerful. ↻

Windows come in all shapes and sizes, and can be installed even in very small spaces. Here, two small square windows help turn a dark attic into an enticing bedroom, providing much-needed light and a bit of fresh air, while also serving as a visual "headboard." The end tables and reading lamps are deliberately unfussy and the white color scheme helps expand the space. ➲

Hidden Assets

Planning ahead is the best way to ensure that your bedroom includes adequate storage. When space is at a premium or simplicity is your goal, **built-in storage** makes sense. Subtle or dramatic, it can form an integral part of the room's design. Built-ins can also let you take advantage of otherwise unused space and tight corners. The best way to get started on your storage plans is to **make a list** of everything you need to stow, and then note how accessible each item needs to be.

bright ideas

▶ Mix and match drawer pulls for a whimsical look

▶ Drawer dividers offer hidden organization

▶ Full extension runners let drawers be pulled all the way out

Plenty of burnished blond wood creates a warm glow in this room. The custom bed platform features drawers underneath, and an adjacent chest of drawers doubles as a nightstand. ➲

When storage is at a premium, an unobtrusive solution is a bed platform with drawers beneath instead of a box spring and mattress bed set. The clean lines of this pale wooden platform bed demonstrate that storage can be sleek and stylish; the matching nightstand provides additional space to stow frequently used items and a surface for things to keep at hand. ➲

Views of the beach on two sides are this bedroom's outstanding features—but storage is still required. The solution here was a practical built-in unit that provides ample storage by combining drawers and cupboards. Drawers are ideal for organizing, while shelves are best for bulkier items. The storage unit was designed to fit beneath the windows, preserving the view, and creates a useful surface for objets and everyday items. ◑

Consider a built-in dresser when space permits. This practical piece was designed to fit perfectly in the space offered by the alcove, taking the place of a freestanding dresser. To maximize storage space, the drawers are extra deep; the surface above becomes a convenient display space for collections and other daily treasures. ↻

Whimsical hardware is a simple way to add charm to built-ins and freestanding pieces alike.

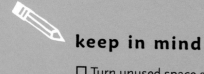

keep in mind

☐ Turn unused space above wardrobes, cabinets, and shelves into display areas

☐ Use accent lighting to highlight collections

A variation on the classic four-poster, this multifaceted bed features a clever overhead shelf to hold books and reading lamps, as well as "secret" storage on either end. The matching nightstands offer additional space for items that need to be easily accessible. ◑

A trunk can be a versatile solution, offering a place to unobtrusively stash extra clothes or linens, a spot to sit, and a decorative element.

A custom wall-to-wall storage unit serves as a combination headboard and nightstand, while providing efficient storage and a convenient shelf for display: an all-in-one design solution! ☊

Get Organized

edroom planners are wise to borrow a page from home-office design. A storage **plan** that combines drawers, shelves, and cabinets will provide an excellent foundation for organizing everything that finds its way into the bedroom, from clothes to books to accessories. Think about creating a **permanent home** for each item. Then it's time to get stylish . . . storage can make a design statement, too.

bright ideas

▶ Install a rod along a side wall of a narrow closet

▶ Add shoe shelves or cubbies

▶ Conceal a built-in hamper behind a cabinet front

A collection of wall-mounted storage boxes is lighthearted and fun. Placed in a deliberately random pattern, the combination of cupboards and drawers stows everything from socks to linens, and the tops of the boxes serve as display space for a collection of hats. ➲

Stacks of books are a frequent problem in bedrooms, yet not every room is enhanced by a standard bookshelf. Here, a U-shaped bay has been outfitted with built-in shelves that follow the curve. The shelving provides ample space below for books, and a convenient display surface above. ◖

This couple decided it was time to eliminate the pile of books growing next to their bed. A simple shelving unit was designed to fit the recessed area above the bed. Cubbies of various sizes accommodate books of different heights and add visual interest. ➲

Break up wall-to-wall books with a decorative object or two.

Customized shelving means that you can tailor your storage solutions to your individual needs and the particulars of your space. In this quirky bedroom, an oval pillar has become a place to stow books up and out of the way. A library ladder provides access and slides all the way around the pillar. ↻

Built-in and custom units create practical storage from unused space.

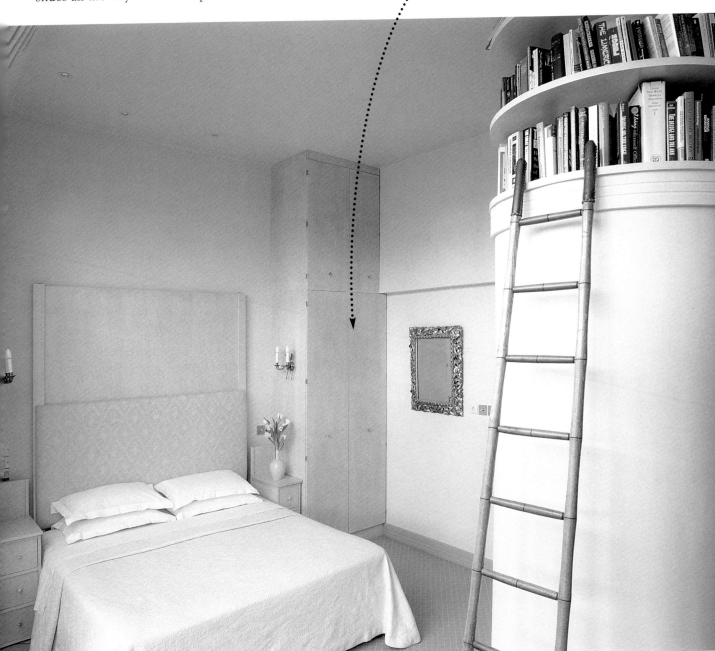

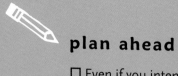

plan ahead

☐ Even if you intend to hire a professional to design your closet, be specific when evaluating your needs: How many pairs of shoes do you have? How many suits? Long dresses? A collection of hats? Sports clothing or equipment?

Well-organized storage areas can relieve stress. This open closet/dressing area incorporates a wall of efficient storage and enough floor space to make trying on clothes a pleasure. The overhead shelf is perfect for boxes of out-of-season clothes, while a combination of drawers and shelves can accommodate a variety of items. ☁

A challenging space is outfitted with a combination of rods, drawers, and open shelves, using every inch of space. Items used most often should be kept at eye-level and within easy reach; stow things used less frequently on higher shelves. ☺

Incorporate a bench or chair into your closet/dressing area when there's room. It's a simple solution worth remembering.

Playing off the exposed beams and pipes, this custom closet was created from glass and wooden shelving and metal poles, all visible through frosted glass panels. It's a closet that bares all, and it is best for people who enjoy being organized. 🎧

An open cupboard provides easy access in a dressing room. Here, wicker baskets transform open shelves into drawer-like storage. The baskets also make an attractive sight. ↻

Note the convenient shelf that stores shoes up and off the ground for easier access.

Rooms with a Hue

An unpainted bedroom is a blank canvas... and the inspirations are infinite. An appealing color scheme may spring from a beautiful set of linens, a favorite print, or the view glimpsed through the window. Walls offer the best opportunity for making a bold (or subtle) color statement, but don't overlook some of the other elements in the room: consider adding color to the ceiling, floors, or furniture.

bright ideas

▶ Add color to the moldings, the window trim, or one wall

▶ Try two shades of the same color for a subtle distinction

▶ Use paint to cover old floors

Multiple colors in a single room can make a bold design statement. Here, a refreshing shade of purple is paired with a soft yellow. The purple serves as a colorful backdrop for the bed, while the yellow provides a gentler contrast. ➲

The different wall colors in this room supply the major visual interest, so simple furniture is the best choice. ⓿

Awash in color and texture, this bedroom is inspired by the hues and fabrics of India. The yellow ochre chosen for the wall behind the bed is offset by an exotic collection of pillows and fabrics in vibrant reds, oranges, and purple. The result is an exotic, sumptuous feast for the eyes. ☉

The point at which two colors meet must be perfectly painted. If you're doing it yourself, mask the adjacent wall to ensure a clean edge.

Hand-dyed Indian cotton sheers in red trimmed with gold are reminiscent of a sari—a bold choice that diffuses the light, casting a warm glow across the room. A swag of fabric draped in a loose canopy above the bed creates an inviting cascade of color. ☊

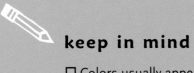

keep in mind

☐ Colors usually appear darker once on the wall; buy a small amount, and try it on the wall before making a final decision

☐ The light, natural and introduced, in a bedroom will also affect the appearance of the color

Paint isn't the only way to add color to walls. Wallpaper provides color, pattern, and texture at the same time. In this eclectic bedroom, subtly striped gold wallpaper is a handsome backdrop for an intricately carved antique bed. ↻

Decorative painting techniques can hide imperfections in walls.

Color need not be solid to be effective. Color washing (applying a diluted color to a neutral base coat with rags, sponges, or brushes) results in a soft, dappled look that adds old-fashioned charm. ➲

The pale hue washed on these walls adds a hint of color but does not compete with the eclectic collection of found furnishings and artwork. ℃

D on't be afraid to use color boldly. In this handsome room, the moss green used on the walls is a key decorative element. ↻

W hite can be used in combination with a bold color to provide contrast. Crisp white linens and accessories accentuate the green walls; the white moldings found throughout the room provide a frame for the stronger color. ↺

Material Dreams

abric offers a fast and often inexpensive way to create a mood or even to change the appearance of a bedroom dramatically. Simple options include updating your bed linens or adding a small but striking touch such as an antique brocade pillow. Fabric can be draped or hung in so many ways: choose a velvet or chenille to create a feeling of luxury and warmth or a breezy sheer to suggest a shimmery coolness.

bright ideas

- Mix and match vintage fabrics for an eclectic look
- Accent fabrics and pillows with decorative fringe and trim
- Blend pattern and texture to make a design statement

Richly patterned and lined with silk, antique damask curtains cordon off a sleeping area. The sleigh bed is dressed in gold linens that coordinate with the draperies at the window. ➲

The gleaming dark wood of this antique bed is set off by the sheer, metallic fabric that surrounds it. Slender metal posts hold a wire from which the draperies hang, allowing the morning light to pass through and transforming the bed into a shimmering refuge. ➲

The appeal of sheer fabric lies in the way it softens a room without obscuring natural light. In this bedroom, a pale fabric is draped loosely from window to window and across the top of the canopy bed, creating an inviting cocoon. ☹

A scarlet patterned fabric anchors the chairs, providing a contrast to the filmy sheers and soft bedclothes.

Pure white paired with neutrals is the recipe for a clean, summery look. Here, white sheers form a romantic canopy above and around the bed. Take note of the shells adorning the pillow shams! ☾

Artfully draped fabric can quickly and inexpensively change the look of a bedroom. Loose loops of sheer fabric envelop and soften this sleek metal bed. ➲

Add texture and a splash of contrasting color with another layer on the bed, such as this lavender chenille blanket.

The bed is the focal point of this spare room, and the fabric is what makes it special. A traditional toile de Jouy is featured on the upholstered headboard, which is a comfortable alternative to wood and conveys a personal touch. The solid bedspread and skirt are neutral counterpoints to all the patterns and textures. ☾

Mix and match fabrics for visual interest. Here, taupe and cream provide a neutral background for the mixed patterns, colors, and textures found in a collection of pillows in varied shapes. ☊

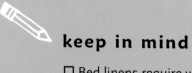

keep in mind

☐ Bed linens require washing—consider care instructions before committing to a duvet, pillow shams, etc.

☐ Direct sunlight will fade fabric. Keep this in mind when selecting fabrics and planning the orientation of your room

In a traditional room characterized by substantial wooden furnishings, an imposing site-built platform bed gets the romantic treatment when it is swathed in a red-and-white toile. Voluminous drapes fall from a fabric-covered valance, and can either be drawn for privacy or held by tiebacks. A matching bedspread and pillow shams complete the rich look. ☻

Fabric can transform more than just the bed. A simple table becomes a luxurious nightstand thanks to a few yards of fabric. The skirt has a kick pleat for easy access to items stowed below. The colors repeat the hues of the duvet cover and shams, creating a unified look. ⟲

A reversible duvet cover allows for a change of decor on a moment's notice. This one features a floral pattern in a warm brick red on one side and a white embroidered design on the other. Pillow shams with contrasting trim work with both looks. ➲

A Question of Style

The inspiration for your bedroom style may come from something as concrete as the architectural details of your home or something as fleeting as the colors of a sunset. Whatever your **passion**, you can create the room of your dreams without professional assistance. Begin by assembling a file of inspirations and resources, and bring it with you whenever you're making **decisions**. In no time, you'll be rejoicing over a perfect find at the flea market or mixing paint colors like a pro.

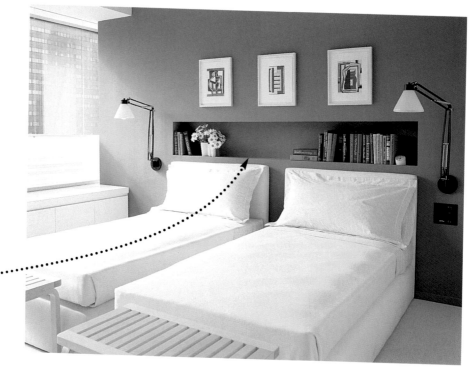

Even a minimalist room requires some storage space. Try a recessed shelf like this one—it also adds architectural interest and a unifying element above the beds.

Clean lines, minimal details, and symmetry give this room its serene style. Two simple white beds flanked by matching lamps rest against a slate-colored wall that also provides a backdrop for the art. 🎧

A passion for modern furniture defines this master bedroom. The substantial platform bed is flanked by two modern masterpieces—the armchair on the left is a Gerrit Rietreld classic, while an Eames rocking armchair sits to the right. A personal collection of design miniatures is displayed along the top of the headboard. ➲

The bedroom as gallery: this handsome room is a contemporary classic that showcases a collection of black-and-white photography. The palette is deliberately neutral so as to avoid overpowering the photographs, which are hung gallery-style around the bed. ☾

Art does not always have to hang on the wall—this drawing rests atop a simple table, forming a vignette with other treasures.

A neutral palette need not be dull: the striped fabric headboard adds subtle color, and a reading lamp with a silvery base echoes the tones of the frames. ☊

Dramatic architecture often calls for simple furnishings. In this room, the spectacular brickwork steals the show. A log bed, plain bedside tables, and a woven rug perform their functions without detracting from the architecture. 🎧

A sense of the past gives this bedroom its unique charm, as its faded walls and worn woodwork are testaments to a long history. An antique bed, graceful in old age, and an elegant rug hanging on the wall complete the picture. 🔊

Why fight the obvious? A rustic log cabin sports exposed logs on its inside walls; two chunky log beds and linens with a pinecone pattern continue the decorating theme. ↻

The landscape may provide all the inspiration necessary. Situated on a rugged coastline, this cottage bedroom's charm comes from stone walls, an exposed wood ceiling, and windows that open to ocean views. Twin beds painted pure white and crisp white linens brighten the room. ➲

A weathered side table contrasts with the smooth, graceful curves of the bed. A handcrafted oil lamp reminds visitors that nature retains the upper hand—perhaps a summer storm will knock out the power. ℮

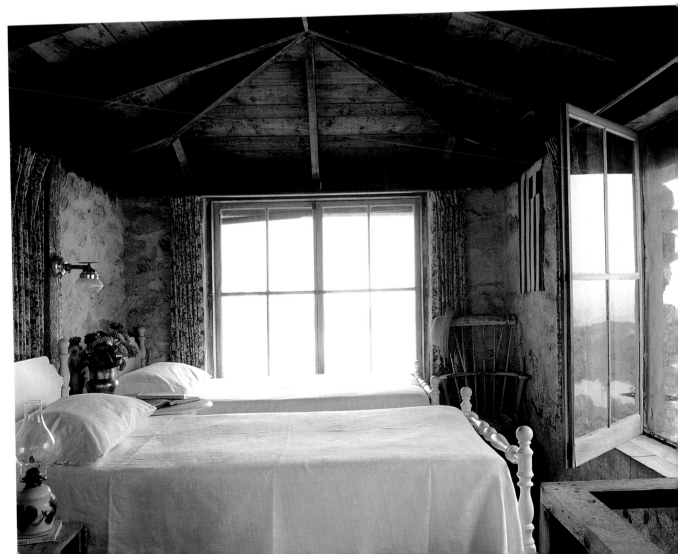

With an imaginative approach, even a standard window can make a statement— this one is dressed up with a lacy sheer.

A small bedroom is transformed into an enchanting Victorian retreat by the magic of chintz and wicker. Flowers are everywhere, from the bed linens that recall vintage fabrics to the collection of botanical prints gracing the handsome green walls. ↻

Romance is always in style in the bedroom. This room achieves its romantic feeling with just a few touches: an antique bed dressed with lacy linens sets the mood, and a handpainted floral design adds a hint of whimsy. ➲

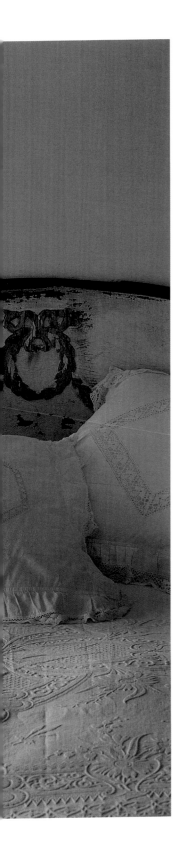

An appreciation for the past is evident in this charming bedroom featuring a headboard fashioned out of an architectural detail. The piece's graceful arc and decorative detailing serve as a beautiful backdrop for a collection of lacy pillows. ☾

Setting the tone in this space is a one-of-a-kind bed featuring a gold-toned frame with an animal-print inset. Just a few unique details—a chandelier-like wall sconce, an ornate mirror, and a gilded side table—give the room an air of sophisticated decadence. ♠

An architecturally unremarkable space is transformed into a thoroughly modern refuge through the careful selection of furnishings, fabric, and art. A curvaceous chair offers a sculptural effect, while a sleek platform bed contributes clean lines and right angles. The photographic triptych above the bed draws the eye upward and helps balance the room. ☻

These curtains make a sculptural statement while blocking out much of the sunlight.

A prized map holds pride of place over the bed, where it is framed perfectly by a niche in the divider.

A custom combination headboard–storage unit creates two distinct areas in this spacious master suite. While the divider is sizable and extremely functional, with storage on either side of the bed, its blond wood and simple design allow the room to retain its light and airy feel. The neutral color scheme and lack of clutter enable the couple's art collection to make the design statement. ◑

Flea market finds provide the telling details of a vintage look in a country bedroom. Faded florals and plaids blend easily on an antique iron bed. ❂

White walls form a pure canvas and create a soothing mood. Add color sparingly to other elements to make a statement. Here, pretty lavender brightens an antique dresser that is framed by sheer curtains in the same hue, while a darker purple graces wood plank floors. ↻

Salvaged items can find new life when used in imaginative ways. This summer cottage brings the outdoors in with picket-fence headboards that grace twin beds united by a real screen door (don't try to open it). ➲

Sweet Dreams

s the most important piece of furniture in the room, the bed often sets the decorative tone for the bedroom. Choose your bed early in the decorating process. You'll be spending a lot of time in it, so you'll want your bed to be **comfortable** and inviting, as well as good-looking. If you're feeling creative, consider designing a **custom** bed or creating a **nontraditional** headboard.

bright ideas

▶ An antique double can be converted to a queen

▶ Trundles accommodate overnight guests

▶ Under-bed drawers offer hidden storage

This iron sconce echoes the headboard without repeating it exactly.

Especially in a small room, finding the wall space for a bed can be a problem. Placing the bed in front of a window is one solution. In this room, the open design of the hand-forged metal headboard lets the light from the window pass through. ♫

This king-size bed is the centerpiece of the bedroom. A majestic upholstered headboard draws the eye, its taupe fabric echoed in the curtains and window blind. Padded headboards make reading in bed especially comfortable. ◐

This one-of-a-kind fanciful bed is the focal point of the room. With its delightful curlicues and different post designs, it commands attention. Pure white bed linens and a plethora of pillows make it inviting, too. ☾

A funky handmade lamp embellished with beads and charms enhances the quirky appeal of this room. ♫

An upholstered headboard turns a ho-hum bed into a comfort zone. It's easy to do: attach a piece of foam to plywood, then cover with the fabric of your choice. Simply bolt the headboard to an ordinary metal bed frame. ➲

A single dowel draped with fabric creates the illusion of a headboard. It's an affordable option that is also flexible—a new fabric can be introduced with each new season! ↻

The simple construction of the "canopy" means that new fabric can create a new look in no time.

Dowels on the ceiling and the wall behind this bed have been draped with fabric to simulate a canopy. In this small room, a sheer blue-and-white check gives a fresh look without overpowering the space. ➲

An ivory color scheme ensures
that the dramatic silhouette
of the bed is not upstaged.

With its high, finial-topped posts and strong
right angles, this sizable bed dominates the room.
Sheer tab curtains on the bed soften the look. ☊

A bench at the base of a bed is highly practical.

Simple yet striking, an Arts and Crafts–inspired tester bed makes a strong design statement. Unadorned by draperies, the bed's rich wood and clean lines stand out. ☊

Rooms with a View

ature's own designs are frequently **breathtaking**: if your bedroom offers a view—be it of a backyard, cityscape, or beach— why not take advantage of it? Oversize windows seem to erase the boundary between outside and in, but even a glimpse of blue skies or greenery can be uplifting. If you are planning to incorporate a **special view**, don't forget to consider issues of privacy. There is such a thing as too much exposure!

bright ideas

▶ Add skylights for a nighttime view of the skies

▶ Double up on windows, vertically

▶ Use adjustable blinds and shades to control light and sun

Walls of glass and doors that open onto a small patio seamlessly integrate this room into its natural surroundings. An overhang protects the patio from the elements and shades the room. ➲

With no neighboring homes, these homeowners opted for a wall of windows—free of drapes—that gives them a clear view of the woods outside while relaxing in bed. Opening a window or two ushers in fresh breezes. ➲

A hot tub turns a bedroom into a spa. The enclosed porch adjoining this master bedroom offers a view of the treetops and features an oversize tub for long, soothing soaks. ↺

Consider the orientation of your bedroom and the amount of direct sunlight you want in the room if you plan a deck.

A private deck is a luxurious addition to a master bedroom. In this spacious room, sheer draperies diffuse some of the sunlight, while a heavier curtain can be drawn when complete privacy is desired. ➲

This bedroom in a summer cottage feels like it's part of the dunes. The lower portion of each window is free of mullions so as to provide maximum enjoyment of the view. A convenient door leads to the deck outside. ☊

Welcoming Guests

omfort and flexibility are the hallmarks of a good guest room. Overnight visitors will appreciate a room that's easy to settle into—generally, that means convenient storage and a comfortable bed. Many guest rooms do double duty as dens or home offices. Think about the ways your spare room will be used, and look for solutions that will make you and your guests feel **right at home.**

bright ideas

▶ Space-saving bunks are fun for young guests

▶ An armoire can conceal an entertainment center

▶ Open shelves make finding things easy

A shelf mounted to the wall behind the bed is a convenient place to make bedtime reading available to guests.

An inviting cottage bedroom dresses up two twin beds as one. It's a smart way to accommodate couples, singles, or kids. Simple hooks on the headboard and footboard latch the two bed frames together, and they can be unhooked just as easily. 🎧

This compact but efficient guest room packs a lot into a small space: a trundle slides out to provide a second bed when more than one guest is expected. A cozy window seat offers a convenient resting place. Built-in shelves and cupboards are easily accessible for quick storage. ☁

A beautiful sleigh bed combines style with function as it easily expands to accommodate two people. In its single state, and with a few throw pillows, it turns into a comfortable place for guests to sit during the day. ☾

Natural materials and a neutral color scheme give this den/guest room a tranquil air. The daybed functions as a sofa until it's time to turn the room over to a guest, at which point simply removing the extra pillows turns it into a comfortable place to sleep. An overhead shelf keeps books out of the way. ☋

An antique trunk stows guest blankets while at the same time serving as a coffee table.

plan ahead

☐ Will guests have a private bathroom, and if so, does it need to be a full bath or will a half-bath do?

☐ Consider an internal and an external entrance for a guest room

A guest room can be the ideal place to indulge in a hobby or special interest. In this room, a love of things nautical has determined the decor, which boasts a collection of model sailboats and paintings of ships. ↺

Mismatched chests painted the same color serve as nightstands and provide storage.

This is a room that grandchildren will love, while adult guests may find that it turns back the clock. The identical twin beds are fancifully architectural, each resting atop a colorful area rug. The airplane motif on the quilts is playful yet not childish. ↻

Entertainment Options

he bedroom is often home to a second television, stereo, or computer, yet finding an **unobtrusive**, efficient place to put it is still a challenge. One solution is an entertainment center. There are plenty of available styles ranging from sleek to traditional, and many provide **convenient** storage. If you're an antique lover, consider adapting an old wardrobe (remember that most electronic equipment will require ventilation, and a section in the back of the wardrobe may have to be cut out).

bright ideas

- ▶ Annex a closet for a computer workstation
- ▶ Plan wiring in advance
- ▶ Wall-mounted speakers are out of the way

The choice of built-ins rather than freestanding pieces makes the most of a relatively small room. A cheerful green stain has been used on all the woodwork, and the corner-mounted television cabinet blends seamlessly with the other components in the room. ⌗

An entertainment center need not hold only electronics; the wooden cabinets on either side of this unit provide convenient storage for clothes and accessories, too.

In this contemporary bedroom, an asymmetrical entertainment center is an integral part of the design. Situated between a floor-to-ceiling window and doors that open to the outside, the piece boasts a simple facade of glass and wood that does not detract from the view. When access to the television is desired, the frosted glass panel slides away. ◑

In this small yet elegantly appointed room, a television in plain view would be out of place. The solution is a handsome cabinet called the "Beehive," which houses electronic equipment and provides discreet storage. Made from American walnut and lined with cedar, the cabinet is designed to hold both a television and a stereo system in its upper level. Its lower level has drawers for clothing storage. ↻

A white cabinet blends easily into the background in this pristine light-filled room. It's an inexpensive option that doesn't command too much attention, yet nevertheless serves a useful dual purpose: housing the television and providing additional storage. ◐

Custom cabinetry is excellent for all kinds of storage; here, chunky night tables and drawers beneath the bed provide hidden space to stash accessories and out-of-season clothing.

The cabinet at the foot of the bed offers the ultimate in unobtrusive entertainment housing— the television set can be summoned to rise from the cabinet by remote control. ➲

Let the Sun Shine In

 well-placed window can make a dramatic difference in a bedroom, bringing in **sunlight** and fresh breezes or offering a glimpse of the stars. Fortunately, windows come in all shapes and sizes, and a solution can be found for just about any space no matter how awkward or unusual. Think about **windows and skylights** as ways to add interesting architectural details to your bedroom.

bright ideas

- A window seat makes a pleasant resting spot
- Incorporate an antique stained-glass window
- Transom windows let light pass through doorways

This circular window becomes a natural headboard, bringing a glimpse of treetops and the glow of natural light into a sleeping loft that might otherwise appear stark. ➲

Adding skylights can make a tremendous difference in a formerly dark room. Shafts of natural light from above change the room's ambience dramatically, and the gleam of moonlight has its own magic. Here, a vaulted ceiling has enough surface area for two large skylights positioned directly over the master bed. ➲

Slats allow control over the amount of light that enters.

When ceilings are high, consider placing windows at different heights to add visual interest to a room. A half-moon window set high on a brilliant blue wall appears to rest atop a canopy bed, which is flanked by two vertical windows. Together, the three windows create an arc of light around the bed. ☾

Details to note include shutters that can be closed and triangular wall sconces that echo the window shape.

In a room with high ceilings but little storage, this couple opted for built-in cabinets on either side of the bed rather than a pair of windows. Their clever solution to the problem of minimal natural light was to tuck in a pair of small triangular windows at ceiling height, letting wedges of daylight into the sleeping area. ➲

A summer bedroom with an exposed ceiling, white beadboard walls, and a sun-filled bay makes for an airy retreat. Large windows facing the beach bring natural light and fresh ocean air indoors. ☊

While the original pair of windows let in some light, this room's occupants yearned for more. A trio of new windows placed just above the headboard was the solution, creating a cheery, sun-splashed space. One relatively simple architectural alteration yielded this dreamy bedroom. ☊

Smart Window Treatments

 ight is a crucial factor in a bedroom. Too much light at the wrong time can ruin **a good night's sleep**; too little light can make a bedroom feel cavelike. The exposure of your bedroom will help to determine the type of window treatment you need. Controlling the amount of light without compromising on good looks is the challenge. The **good news** is that there are plenty of options that combine function with style!

bright ideas

▶ Shutters create an antique effect

▶ Sheers keep it light and airy

▶ Opaque blinds let in some light but maintain privacy

A simple pulley system raises the shade to cover the window.

Three problems beset this elegant, minimal bedroom: a single small window above an unattractive radiator was set into a slanted outside wall. The solution was to install a traditional pull-down shade in the window frame, then to mount a sheer pull-up shade to the floor behind a wood valance. A maximum of the available light can now enter, the radiator is covered, and privacy is no problem. 𝄒

A semicircular window is the focal point of this sleeping loft, becoming a light-filled headboard for the unadorned bed. When windows make a strong architectural statement, they don't need a complicated treatment. A simple shade mounted on the wall above can be lowered at night, yet is nearly invisible when rolled. ↻

This tranquil bedroom features voluminous curtain panels in a traditional style paired with white sheers that let just the right amount of light pass through. Heavier fabrics will block out the light, provide complete privacy when desired, and help muffle city noises. The monochromatic scheme of the room is soothing and peaceful, while the combination of fabrics and textures found on the bed, furnishings, and window treatments contributes to restful repose. ◑

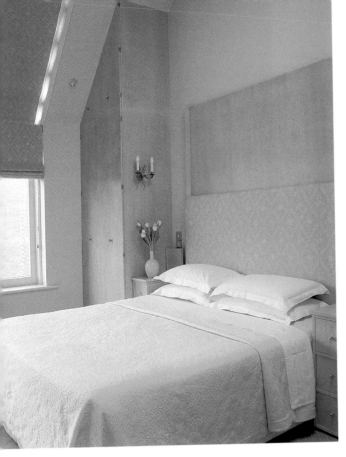

A window flows directly into a skylight in this bedroom with a soaring ceiling. The elongated roman shade was custom designed, and can be raised or lowered depending on the amount of light desired. ☾

Much of this small room's charm comes from the combination of layers and textures. A bamboo blind is an interesting choice that lets in light while providing its own visual interest. Another layer—this one made up of sheer fabric panels—hangs from a rod mounted above the window. These romantic sheers can be drawn to create a more dramatic effect. ➲

A large bay area with a desk and a comfortable armchair has three generous windows that let the natural light pour into this bedroom. The natural blinds filter but do not block the light even when they are lowered. ⏻

Note that there are no rugs covering these beautiful wood floors—direct sunlight will fade carpets and bed linens.

An all-white bedroom maximizes the natural light from windows that wrap right around the corner of the room. Simple white shades complement the woven headboard and wainscoting, and almost disappear completely when they are rolled tight. ☻

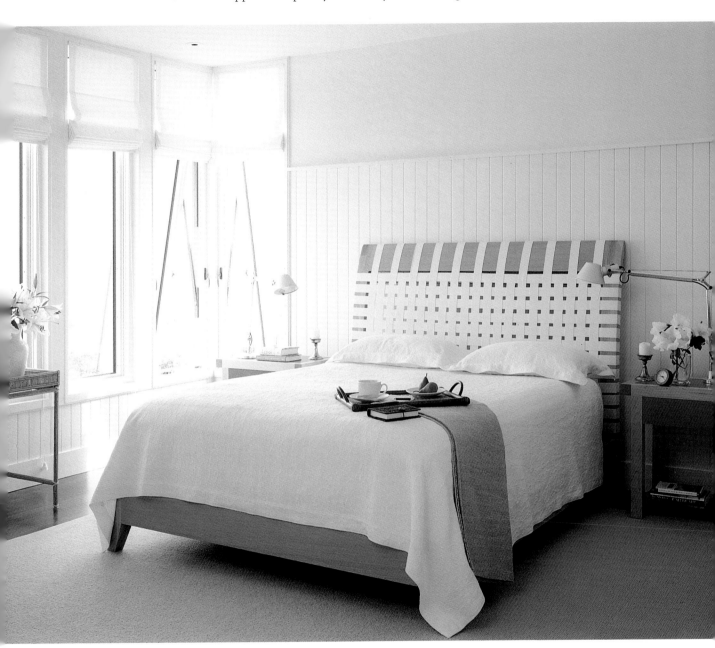

Lights Out

Natural light is only half the bedroom story: what happens at night? A bedroom may require several different lighting solutions to ensure overall **illumination** of the room, as well as adequate light for tasks like reading in bed. Lighting is also a decorative element and a major source of **ambience**.

Light from an adjacent room filters through the sliding screens and the louvered panels above them.

bright ideas

▶ Recessed bulbs to spotlight areas with a direct beam

▶ Multiple controls—at entrance and bedside

▶ Closet lighting

A good bedside lamp should illuminate the reading area without brightening the entire room. Here, a pair of stylish fixtures has been mounted to the wall within easy reach of the bed. Their shades can be adjusted to redirect the light where it's needed. ➲

Lighting can make a dramatic decorative statement, as in this Japanese-style bedroom, in which lighting decisions were an integral part of the design process. The bed is recessed into a shallow niche with lighting built in above and on the sides. Panel lights cast a warm glow, while pinpoint spots provide direct light for reading. ➲

With no overhead lighting, only the soft glow of lamps illuminates this minimal bedroom. In keeping with the room's spare yet comfortable feel, the bedside lamp is a simple cylinder that takes on a sculptural form when illuminated. A small desk also requires lighting: a base with clean lines is topped by a cylindrical shade that echoes the design of the bedside lamp.

Fresh flowers are lovely near the bed. A small silver vase complements the lamp and creates an attractive still life.

When selecting a bedside lamp, it's important to think about the style and scale of nearby furnishings. A classic silver-plated lamp is a delicate accompaniment to the graceful bed and slender nightstand in this room. ⊂

A traditional brass lamp is mounted to the wall next to the bed, leaving more room on the nightstand for items such as a clock, a book, and a vase of fresh flowers. This lamp swings out from the wall and can be brought closer to the bed thanks to a jointed arm. ➲

Ceiling fans help keep air circulating, and are available in many styles with and without lighting.

Bedside lighting doesn't have to be expensive or require complicated installation. In this retro bedroom, a simple desk lamp is re-purposed to serve as a reading lamp. Its adjustable arm makes it well suited to the task, while its simple styling and bright color work with the modern touches in the room, including the vintage patterned bedspread and Marcel Breuer nesting tables. ➲

Consider highlighting a special collection or interesting architectural detail in your bedroom. In this spacious room, three large botanical prints are illuminated with spots from above. ◑

Resources

Information and Products

If you are interested in hiring a qualified professional to help with a remodeling job or new construction, here is a list of design and planning resources that may be helpful:

American Institute of Architects (AIA)—When making structural changes, an architect should be considered. Many, but not all, architects belong to The American Institute of Architects. Call (202) 626-7300 for information and the phone number of your local chapter. www.aiaonline.com

The American Society of Interior Designers (ASID)—An interior designer can provide helpful advice, especially when remodeling an existing space. The American Society of Interior Designers represents over 20,000 professionally qualified interior designers. Call ASID's client/referral service at (800) 775-ASID. www.asid.org

National Association of the Remodeling Industry (NARI)—When it's time to select a contractor to work on your project, you might consider a member of the National Association of the Remodeling Industry. Call (800) 611-6274 for more information. www.nari.org

National Association of Home Builders (NAHB)—When you're looking at builders to construct a new home, contact the National Association of Home Builders. Call (800) 368-5242 for more information. www.nahb.org

The following manufacturers, associations, and resources may be helpful as you plan your bedroom:

GENERAL

Home Depot
(800) 430-3376
www.homedepot.com

Lowe's
(800) 44-LOWES
www.lowes.com

FABRIC & WALL COVERINGS

Brunschwig & Fils
www.brunschwig.com

Eisenhart Wall Coverings
(800) 726-3267

Imperial Wall Coverings
(800) 539-5399
www.imp-wall.com

Waverly
(800) 423-5881
www.waverly.com

FLOORING

www.floorfacts.com
(a global directory that helps consumers explore flooring options)

Italian Trade Commission
Ceramic Tile Department
499 Park Avenue
New York, NY 10022
(212) 980-1500
www.italtrade.com

National Wood Flooring
  Association
16388 Westwoods Business
  Park
Ellisville, MO 63021
(800) 422-4556
www.woodfloors.org

Trade Commission of Spain
Ceramic Tile Department
2655 Le Jeune Road, Suite 114
Coral Gables, FL 33134
(305) 446-4387
www.tilespain.com

FURNISHINGS, LINENS, AND ACCESSORIES

Arhaus
(866) 427-4287
www.arhaus.com

Baker Furniture
(800) 59-BAKER
www.bakerfurniture.com

Century Furniture
(828) 328-1851
www.centuryfurniture.com

Chambers
www.chamberscatalog.com

Charles P. Rogers Beds
(800) 272-7726
www.charlesprogers.com

Crate & Barrel
(800) 967-6696
www.crateandbarrel.com

Ethan Allen
(800) 228-9229
www.ethanallen.com

Garnet Hill
(800) 622-6216
www.garnethill.com

Harden Furniture
(315) 245-1000
www.harden.com

Ikea
(800) 225-IKEA
www.ikea.com

Lands' End
(800) 963-4816
www.landsend.com

Lexington Home Furnishings
(800) 539-4636
www.lexington.com

L.L. Bean
(800) 441-5713
www.llbean.com

Mitchell Gold Company
(800) 789-5401
www.mitchellgold.com

Pottery Barn
(800) 922-5507
www.potterybarn.com

Room & Board
(800) 486-6554
www.roomandboard.com

Rowe Furniture
(800) 334-7693
www.rowefurniture.com

Sauder Furniture
(800) 523-3987
www.sauder.com

Scott Jordan Furniture
(212) 620-4682
www.scottjordan.com

Spiegel
(800) SPIEGEL
www.spiegel.com